FREE AND FEARLESS

WALKING BOLDLY IN THE LOVE THAT HEALS
SHORT BIBLE STUDY

From The Author of Overcoming Abuse God's Way

JANET MARIE NAPPER

Free and Fearless: Walking Boldly in the Love that Heals

Copyright © 2025 Janet Marie Napper for Overcoming Abuse God's Way

ALL RIGHTS RESERVED.

No portion of this book may be reproduced in any form without permission from the publisher except as permitted by US Copyright Law. For permissions, contact: order@speaktruthmedia.com.

All scripture references in this book are taken from the *Holy Bible*, New Living Translation, Copyright © 1996, 2004, 2015 by Tyndale House Foundation. Used by permission of Tyndale House Publishers, Inc., Carol Stream, Illinois 60188. All rights reserved.

AI-Assistance Disclosure

This workbook was prayerfully written and authored by Janet Marie Napper. Portions of the content were refined with the assistance of AI editing tools to enhance clarity, structure, and readability. All biblical insight, personal testimony, and ministry teaching reflect the author's original message, experiences, and life's work as presented in Overcoming Abuse God's Way: Rags to Riches. No portion of this work was generated without the author's review, guidance, and approval.

Cover design: Janet Marie Napper for Overcoming Abuse God's Way

Published by: SpeakTruth Media Group LLC

ISBN: 979-8-218-92657-1

Printed in USA – First Edition

Dedication

To my Lord and Savior, Jesus Christ.

To the One who loved me first,
the One who gave me freedom to believe I have value and purpose,
The One whose faithfulness made me fearless in my journey of healing and restoration from physical, sexual, emotional, verbal, and financial abuse. You are mine, and I am Yours.

If He could do it for me, He can do it for you.   — *Janet Marie Napper*

Table of Contents

Introduction: A Message of Hope 6

Lesson 1: What Is Abuse 7

Lesson 2: Abuse Profiles 10

Lesson 3: Love is Love & Arrested Development 13

Lesson 4: Spirit, Soul, Body 16

Lesson 5: How God Meets Our Needs 19

Lesson 6: Pain, Addiction, & the Pain Cycle 23

Lesson 7: Fear 26

Lesson 8: Rejection 29

Lesson 9: Judging 32

Lesson 10: Anger 36

Lesson 11: Forgiveness 39

Lesson 12: Loving Others & Blended Families 42

Lesson 13: Codependency 45

Lesson 14: Romance & Sexual Addiction 48

Lesson 15: Generational Patterns & Ancestral Sin 52

Lesson 16: Root Strongholds Soul Ties 56

A note from Janet Marie Napper 67

Material Resources 68

A Message of Hope

You were created for more—more than survival, more than silent suffering, more than merely getting by. You were made in the image of a loving God, whose endless love reaches into every broken place, every painful memory, and every hidden wound.

This workbook is not just a study. It is a **journey of healing**, rooted in biblical truth, carried by grace, and led by the One who promises to restore what was lost with insights from Janet Marie Napper's book Overcoming Abuse God's Way: Rags to Riches

God's love is not just for eternity—it begins **here and now**. He cares for your **spirit**, your **soul**, and your **body**. He wants to bring freedom from the pain of childhood abuse, the shame of past decisions, and the confusion of relationship wounds. In Him, you can find **identity**, **purpose**, and **peace**.

For those who have experienced emotional, physical, spiritual, or sexual abuse—this study gently uncovers the lies you may have believed and replaces them with the **life-giving truth** of God's Word. It shows how trauma impacts our choices and relationships—and how God's love rebuilds what was torn down.

You'll discover that healing is possible, learn to walk in forgiveness, confront strongholds, and understand why you feel the way you do. Whether you are beginning this journey or walking alongside someone who is, know this:

You are not alone. You are deeply loved. And your story is not over.

One day, we will step into eternity—where God will wipe away every tear and all sorrow will be no more. But until then, this is a sacred invitation to live whole and free, **starting now**.

Let this be your new beginning.

Lesson 1: What Is Abuse?

Introduction

Abuse is a violation of the image of God in another human being. It involves using power, control, or manipulation to harm another person emotionally, physically, verbally, spiritually, sexually, or financially. Whether experienced in childhood, marriage, relationships, or family, abuse leaves deep scars—but God offers restoration. Understanding what abuse is, from a biblical perspective, is the first step toward healing.

Biblical Foundation: Tamar's Story (2 Samuel 13)

One of the most heartbreaking stories in the Bible is found in 2 Samuel 13. Tamar, daughter of King David, was abused by someone she trusted—her own half-brother, Amnon. This story reveals the manipulation, violation, and emotional devastation that abuse causes. It also shows God's Word does not shy away from real pain. He sees, He cares, and He redeems.

Scripture (NLT)

"But Tamar was a very beautiful woman, and Amnon became so obsessed with her that he became ill. She was a virgin, and Amnon thought he could never have her."
— 2 Samuel 13:2 (NLT)

"Well then," Amnon said, "bring the food into my bedroom and feed it to me here." So Tamar took his favorite dish to him. But as she was feeding him, he grabbed her and demanded, "Come to bed with me, my darling sister!"
"No, my brother!" she cried. "Don't be foolish! Don't do this to me! Such wicked things aren't done in Israel. Where could I go in my shame? And you would be called one of the greatest fools in Israel. Please, just speak to the king about it, and he will let you marry me."
But Amnon wouldn't listen to her, and since he was stronger than she was, he raped her. Then suddenly Amnon's love turned to hate, and he hated her even more than he had loved her. "Get out of here!" he snarled at her.
"No, no!" Tamar cried. "Sending me away now is worse than what you've already done to me."

But Amnon wouldn't listen to her. He shouted for his servant and demanded, "Throw this woman out, and lock the door behind her!"
– 2 Samuel 13:10–17 (NLT)

Life Application

Like Tamar, many survivors have been violated, silenced, or discarded. Abuse causes deep emotional confusion and spiritual injury. But God does not ignore the cries of the brokenhearted. Psalm 34:18 tells us, *"The Lord is close to the brokenhearted; he rescues those whose spirits are crushed."* Abuse is never your fault. The path to healing begins with truth—acknowledging the wrong, breaking the silence, and allowing God's Word to restore your worth.

Group Discussion Questions

1. How has Tamar's story helped you see that abuse is not your fault?
2. What forms of abuse have you or others experienced that are often overlooked (verbal, emotional, spiritual)?
3. What do you think God feels when someone is mistreated or abused?
4. What small but brave step can you take today to move toward healing?

Child-Sensitive Note

If adapting this for younger audiences (ages 10–15), use language like *"being hurt or treated unfairly by someone who should love or protect you."* Explain that God never wants us to be hurt and always provides safe people to help. Encourage children to talk to a trusted adult and remind them they are never alone.

Closing Prayer

Gracious Father,
Thank You for being a God who sees, who heals, and who restores. Just as You saw Tamar in her pain, You see each of us in ours. We lift every heart wounded by abuse and ask for Your comfort, strength, and peace. Heal the broken places, silence the lies of shame, and

remind us of the truth that we are loved, valued, and created in Your image. Give us the courage to take steps toward freedom and surround us with people who reflect Your love and care. May Your Word continue to be our guide and Your Spirit our comforter as we walk the path of healing. In Jesus' precious name, Amen.

Author's Note

Janet shares that abuse is not only about the harm done but also about the lies it plants deep in the heart. Her testimony reminds us that while abuse may leave scars, God's truth has the final word—declaring His children loved, worthy, and destined for restoration.

Excerpt adapted with permission from Janet Marie Napper's personal story, **Overcoming Abuse God's Way: Rags to Riches.**

Lesson 2: Abuse Profiles

Introduction

Abuse doesn't always look the same. Some wounds are visible, but many go unseen. Abuse can be emotional, verbal, physical, sexual, spiritual, or financial. Understanding the different types of abuse helps us identify past harm and begin the journey to healing. This awareness also allows us to recognize red flags in relationships and set healthy boundaries.

Common Abuse Profiles

- **Emotional Abuse** – Manipulation, control, intimidation, or constant criticism that damages self-worth.

- **Verbal Abuse** – Name-calling, yelling, shaming, or threats that create fear or destroy confidence.

- **Physical Abuse** – Harming or threatening to harm someone physically (hitting, grabbing, restraining).

- **Sexual Abuse** – Any unwanted sexual activity, including coercion, exploitation, or assault.

- **Spiritual Abuse** – Using faith, Scripture, or religious authority to manipulate, control, or shame.

- **Financial Abuse** – Withholding money, stealing, or using finances to control someone's freedom.

Biblical Foundation: Abigail and Nabal (1 Samuel 25)

Abigail was a wise and godly woman married to a harsh and abusive man named Nabal. Scripture says he was *"crude and mean in all his dealings."* When David's men asked Nabal for food during a time of peace, Nabal insulted them, risking everyone's safety. Abigail humbly intervened to protect her household—demonstrating courage, wisdom, and peacekeeping, even in a toxic marriage.

Scripture (NLT)

"There was a wealthy man from Maon who owned property near the town of Carmel. He had 3,000 sheep and 1,000 goats, and it was time for sheep-shearing. This man's name was Nabal, and his wife, Abigail, was a sensible and beautiful woman. But Nabal, a descendant of Caleb, was crude and mean in all his dealings."
– 1 Samuel 25:2–3 (NLT)

"David's young men gave this message to Nabal in David's name, and they waited for a reply. 'Who is this fellow David?' Nabal sneered. 'Who does this son of Jesse think he is?'"
– 1 Samuel 25:9–10 (NLT)

"Abigail wasted no time. She quickly gathered 200 loaves of bread, two wineskins full of wine, five sheep that had been slaughtered… and she rode her donkey to meet David."
– 1 Samuel 25:18–20 (NLT)

Life Application

Abigail's story shows that living with an abusive or foolish person can put everyone at risk. But God honors wisdom, humility, and courage. Whether the abuse is loud and violent or quiet and controlling, God sees the pain. He calls us to truth, healing, and sometimes, intervention. Understanding abuse profiles gives us language for our pain and helps us take wise steps toward safety and recovery.

Group Discussion Questions

1. Which type of abuse (emotional, verbal, etc.) do you feel is often ignored or misunderstood?
2. Have you ever felt like Abigail—caught in a toxic or fearful environment?
3. What steps of wisdom did Abigail take that we can learn from today?
4. How can we support others who may still be living in abusive relationships?

Child-Sensitive Note

When helping younger teens understand abuse profiles, use simple terms like *"being treated in ways that hurt your feelings, body, or safety."* Let them know that healthy love never makes them feel scared, small, or worthless. Encourage them to speak to a trusted adult if anything feels wrong or confusing.

Closing Prayer

Heavenly Father,

We thank You for the wisdom found in Your Word and for the example of Abigail, who showed courage and discernment in the face of cruelty. Lord, we lift up every person who has experienced emotional, verbal, physical, sexual, spiritual, or financial abuse. You see every hidden wound and hear every unspoken cry. Bring Your healing touch where there is brokenness, and replace fear with Your peace. Give us wisdom to recognize abuse, courage to set healthy boundaries, and strength to walk in Your truth. Surround us with safe, godly people who will encourage and protect us. May Your love restore our worth and remind us daily that we are precious in Your sight. In Jesus' name, Amen.

Author's Note

Janet shares that abuse often hides behind closed doors—sometimes with words, sometimes in silence, sometimes through control. In her own journey, she discovered that naming the abuse for what it was brought freedom and light into dark places. Her testimony is a reminder that God not only heals the visible wounds but also restores the broken identity that abuse tries to

Excerpt adapted with permission from Janet Marie Napper's personal story, ***Overcoming Abuse God's Way: Rags to Riches.***

Lesson 3: What Is Love & Arrested Development

Introduction

Love is one of our deepest needs—but many survivors of abuse struggle to understand or receive it. Abuse can distort the meaning of love, making it feel unsafe, conditional, or even manipulative. When love is misunderstood in childhood, emotional growth can be stunted. This is called **arrested development**—when trauma freezes a part of us in immaturity, leaving us insecure, fear-based, or trapped in a victim mentality. True healing begins by experiencing God's love, which is perfect, unconditional, and unchanging.

Biblical Foundation: Hosea and Gomer (Hosea 1–3)

The prophet Hosea's marriage to Gomer is a striking picture of God's love. Gomer repeatedly abandoned Hosea for destructive relationships, yet Hosea pursued her in obedience to God, buying her back from bondage. This story reveals the heart of God's love—faithful, sacrificial, and unrelenting—even when we are broken, unfaithful, or unable to love well in return.

Scripture (NLT)

"When the Lord first began speaking to Israel through Hosea, he said to him, 'Go and marry a prostitute, so that some of her children will be conceived in prostitution. This will illustrate how Israel has acted like a prostitute by turning against the Lord and worshiping other gods.'"
— Hosea 1:2 (NLT)

"Then the Lord said to me, 'Go and love your wife again, even though she commits adultery with another lover. This will illustrate that the Lord still loves Israel, even though the people have turned to other gods and love to worship them.' So I bought her back for fifteen pieces of silver and five bushels of barley and a measure of wine."
— Hosea 3:1–2 (NLT)

Life Application

Abuse often teaches us a false definition of love—that it is earned, manipulated, or withdrawn when we fail. But God's love is completely different. It is steady, unconditional, and healing. Without understanding God's love, many survivors remain emotionally insecure or stuck in arrested development—responding like a frightened child instead of a confident adult.

Healing requires two steps:

1. **Receiving God's love** – believing His Word that you are valuable, chosen, and deeply loved.
2. **Growing in maturity** – allowing His Spirit to renew your mind, heal your emotions, and strengthen your identity.

As Hosea loved Gomer faithfully, God loves us—even in our brokenness. His love gives us the security we never had and the power to grow into the person He created us to be.

Group Discussion Questions

1. What false definitions of love have you experienced because of abuse?
2. How does God's love, shown in Hosea's story, look different from human love?
3. Can you identify areas in your life where abuse has caused you to feel emotionally "stuck"?
4. What steps can help you begin to grow past arrested development into maturity with God's help?

Child-Sensitive Note

For younger audiences, explain love as: *"Love means being cared for in a safe way that helps you grow."* Sometimes, when people are hurt as kids, a part of them feels "stuck" at that age. But God's love helps us grow strong and confident again. Encourage children to know that God's love never changes, even if people's love does.

Closing Prayer

Heavenly Father,

Thank You for showing us what real love looks like. Many of us have been given a false picture of love through pain, rejection, or abuse. Lord, heal the places in our hearts where we feel unloved or stuck in fear. Help us to grow beyond arrested development and into the maturity You desire for us. Surround us with people who reflect Your love, and remind us that we are safe in Your arms. Thank You for loving us faithfully, unconditionally, and without end. In Jesus' name, Amen.

Author's Note

Janet writes that as a child of abuse, she struggled to understand love. What she received felt conditional and unsafe, leaving her insecure and fearful. Abuse froze parts of her heart in immaturity, causing her to respond from pain rather than freedom. But when she encountered God's love, she discovered it was not based on performance, but on who she was in Him. His love gave her the strength to grow, mature, and live free from the lies of abuse.

Excerpt adapted with permission from Janet Marie Napper's personal story, ***Overcoming Abuse God's Way: Rags to Riches.***

Lesson 4: Spirit, Soul, and Body

Introduction

God created us with three parts—spirit, soul, and body. Abuse often distorts how we see ourselves and how we live in these areas. When our identity is harmed by trauma, we may look for comfort in unhealthy attachments or coping mechanisms. But God designed each part of us for His purpose: our spirit to know Him, our soul to think and feel truth, and our body to experience His creation. Understanding who we are in Christ is essential to healing and transformation.

Biblical Foundation: Paul's Teaching on Wholeness (1 Thessalonians 5:23)

Paul prayed that believers would be kept blameless in spirit, soul, and body. This shows us that God cares about the wholeness of every part of our being. Abuse affects the whole person, but God's restoration also reaches every part.

Scripture (NLT)

"Now may the God of peace make you holy in every way, and may your whole spirit and soul and body be kept blameless until our Lord Jesus Christ comes again."
– 1 Thessalonians 5:23 (NLT)

"For the word of God is alive and powerful. It is sharper than the sharpest two-edged sword, cutting between soul and spirit, between joint and marrow. It exposes our innermost thoughts and desires."
– Hebrews 4:12 (NLT)

Life Application

- **Spirit** – The spirit is created to worship and know God. But when we've been abused, our spirit can become misdirected toward harmful attachments that feel familiar. Instead of intimacy with God, survivors may seek connection through addiction, unhealthy relationships, or destructive patterns. God calls our spirit back to Himself, where true belonging and safety are found.

- **Soul** – The soul is our mind, emotions, and will. Abuse fills the soul with lies, fear, and shame. Survivors may believe they are worthless or powerless. The truth is, *we have the power to think what we want, but what we think has power over us.*

Healing involves renewing our minds with God's Word, learning to manage emotions in healthy ways, and choosing His truth over past lies.

- **Body** – The body is the temple of the Holy Spirit. It allows us to enjoy God's creation, but it can also be misused through trauma or addictive behaviors. Some turn to romance, sexual sin, or other addictions to fill the emptiness. God restores dignity and purpose to our bodies, calling us to honor Him with what we do and how we live.

God's restoration means wholeness—spirit alive to Him, soul healed in His truth, and body strengthened to walk in freedom.

Group Discussion Questions

1. Which part of your being—spirit, soul, or body—do you feel has been most affected by abuse?
2. What lies have you believed about yourself, and how does God's Word correct those lies?
3. How does renewing the mind help us avoid being "triggered" by memories?
4. What practical steps can you take to honor God with your spirit, soul, and body this week?

Child-Sensitive Note

Explain that God made us with three parts: our spirit (the part that talks to God), our soul (our thoughts and feelings), and our body (what we live in every day). When someone hurts us, all three parts can feel pain. But God heals every part of us. Tell children: *"God made you special in every way. He cares about how you feel, what you think, and what happens to your body. He wants you to be safe and whole."*

Closing Prayer

Lord God,
You created us in Your image—spirit, soul, and body. We confess that abuse has wounded us deeply in every part of who we are. But we thank You that Your healing is greater than the pain. Restore our spirits to worship You, renew our souls with Your truth, and strengthen our bodies to walk in freedom. Help us to live in the fullness of who

You created us to be. Surround us with Your peace and remind us daily that we belong to You. In Jesus' name, Amen.

Author's Note

Janet shares that abuse left her spirit searching for love in unhealthy places, her soul filled with lies and fear, and her body carrying the weight of pain and coping behaviors. She testifies that God's truth became the anchor that restored her whole being. As she learned to separate the lies from God's Word, she discovered freedom: her spirit could worship again, her soul could find peace, and her body could walk in dignity. Her story is proof that God brings wholeness to every part of us.

Excerpt adapted with permission from Janet Marie Napper's personal story, **Overcoming Abuse God's Way: Rags to Riches.**

Lesson 5: How God Meets Our Needs

Introduction

God created each of us with unique gifts, talents, and a divine purpose. But before we can walk in that purpose, our basic needs must be met. Abuse often leaves these needs unmet, distorted, or replaced with harmful substitutes. Healing begins when we learn that God Himself is the One who provides for every need—physical, personal, and spiritual. He not only meets those needs but also restores our identity and shows us how valuable we are to Him.

Biblical Foundation: God Provides for Elijah (1 Kings 17)

When Elijah was weary and in danger, God provided for him supernaturally. At the Kerith Brook, Elijah was given food and water. Later, during famine, God sent him to a widow's home where provision continued. This story reveals that God sees our needs and faithfully provides for them in every season of life.

Scripture (NLT)

"Then the Lord said to Elijah, 'Go to the east and hide by Kerith Brook, near where it enters the Jordan River. Drink from the brook and eat what the ravens bring you, for I have commanded them to bring you food.' So Elijah did as the Lord told him and camped beside Kerith Brook east of the Jordan. The ravens brought him bread and meat each morning and evening, and he drank from the brook."
— 1 Kings 17:2–6 (NLT)

Life Application

God meets our needs in order:

1. **Physical Needs** – Food, water, shelter, and safety. Abuse can rob survivors of these basics, creating fear of survival. But God promises provision, just as He cared for Elijah.

    - *"And this same God who takes care of me will supply all your needs from his glorious riches, which have been given to us in Christ Jesus."* (Philippians 4:19 NLT)

2. **Personal Needs** – These go deeper than survival. Every person longs to feel:
    - **Importance** – knowing we matter to God and others.
    - **Forgiveness** – being freed from guilt and shame.
    - **Acceptance** – belonging and being loved as we are.
    - **Purpose** – living with meaning and direction.

Abuse often attacks these areas, leaving survivors feeling worthless or unseen. But God's Word restores each one:

- *"I have loved you, my people, with an everlasting love. With unfailing love I have drawn you to myself."* (Jeremiah 31:3 NLT)
- *"Even before he made the world, God loved us and chose us in Christ to be holy and without fault in his eyes."* (Ephesians 1:4 NLT)
- *"For we are God's masterpiece. He has created us anew in Christ Jesus, so we can do the good things he planned for us long ago."* (Ephesians 2:10 NLT)

3. **Spiritual Needs** – Our deepest need is to love God and love others. Once physical and personal needs are met, healing allows us to fulfill this greatest commandment. Abuse often distorts our view of God, but His Word restores relationship and trust.

    - *"'You must love the Lord your God with all your heart, all your soul, and all your mind.' This is the first and greatest commandment. A second is equally important: 'Love your neighbor as yourself.'"* (Matthew 22:37–39 NLT)

When survivors realize that God values them—not because of possessions, education, or status, but simply because they are His beloved children—they begin to walk in truth and freedom.

Group Discussion Questions

1. Which of your needs (physical, personal, or spiritual) has felt most neglected or attacked through abuse?

2. How does Elijah's story encourage you about God's provision in your life?

3. Which personal need (importance, forgiveness, acceptance, purpose) speaks most strongly to where you are right now?

4. How can receiving God's love in these areas prepare you to love Him and others more fully?

Child-Sensitive Note

Explain needs simply: *"We all need food, water, and a safe place to live. We also need to feel loved, important, and forgiven. God gives us these things because He loves us."* For children, use Elijah's story: *"God even sent birds to bring Elijah food! That's how much God cares."* Encourage kids to see that God cares about every part of their lives.

Closing Prayer

Heavenly Father,
Thank You that You care about every one of our needs. Thank You for providing food, water, and safety, just as You did for Elijah. Thank You for giving us love, acceptance, forgiveness, importance, and purpose. Lord, heal the places where abuse left us feeling empty or unworthy. Teach us to receive Your love and to walk in the truth that we are valuable in Your eyes. Help us to trust that You will always meet our needs and guide us into the purpose You created us for. In Jesus' name, Amen.

Author's Note

Janet recalls seasons when even basic needs felt uncertain because of the chaos of abuse. Yet she discovered that God was her Provider, meeting physical needs in miraculous ways, surrounding her with people who showed love, and restoring her sense of **importance, forgiveness, acceptance, and purpose**. She testifies that walking in God's truth transforms survival into abundant life—because when He meets your needs, you learn that you are never forgotten and always cherished.

Excerpt adapted with permission from Janet Marie Napper's personal story, **Overcoming Abuse God's Way: Rags to Riches.**

Lesson 6: Pain, Addiction, and the Pain Cycle

Introduction

Pain doesn't just go away. When we don't have healthy ways to deal with it, we often find unhealthy ways to survive. This is how the pain cycle begins. Abuse, rejection, or trauma creates deep wounds—and in trying to numb the pain, we may turn to addictions: food, fantasy, romance, social media, drugs, people-pleasing, or withdrawal. But the more we try to fix ourselves, the more trapped we feel. The good news is: Jesus came to break the cycle of pain, shame, and striving.

Biblical Foundation: The Bleeding Woman (Mark 5:25–34)

This woman lived in pain for twelve years. She had spent all her money trying to get better, yet her condition only worsened. She likely felt ashamed, isolated, and hopeless. But something inside her still believed she could be healed. When she reached out in faith—quietly, humbly—Jesus not only healed her body, He restored her dignity.

Scripture (NLT)

"A woman in the crowd had suffered for twelve years with constant bleeding. She had suffered a great deal from many doctors, and over the years she had spent everything she had to pay them, but she had gotten no better. In fact, she had gotten worse."

"She had heard about Jesus, so she came up behind him through the crowd and touched his robe. For she thought to herself, 'If I can just touch his robe, I will be healed.'"

"Immediately the bleeding stopped, and she could feel in her body that she had been healed of her terrible condition."

"Jesus realized at once that healing power had gone out from him, so he turned around in the crowd and asked, 'Who touched my robe?'"

"Then the frightened woman, trembling at the realization of what had happened to her, came and fell to her knees in front of him and told him what she had done. And he said to her, 'Daughter, your faith has made you well. Go in peace. Your suffering is over.'"
– Mark 5:25–34 (NLT)

Life Application

Like the woman in this story, many of us have suffered silently for years. We've tried to fix ourselves or hide our pain. Addiction is often not about the substance or behavior—it's about trying to ease what feels unbearable.

Common pain responses include:

- Food or comfort eating
- Romance or fantasy
- Social media scrolling
- Alcohol or drugs
- Sexual addiction or co-dependency
- Withdrawal and isolation

These coping mechanisms may bring temporary relief but leave us emptier and more ashamed. God sees it all. And still, He invites us to reach out to Him. When we touch Jesus with honesty and faith, He doesn't shame us. He heals, restores, and calls us *daughter, son, beloved.*

Group Discussion Questions

1. What kinds of pain have you carried silently, like the bleeding woman?
2. Have you ever tried to fix yourself with things that only made you feel worse?
3. What did it take for the woman to reach out to Jesus? What might it take for you?
4. What do you hear Jesus saying to you today as you bring Him your pain?

Child-Sensitive Note

When explaining pain and coping to younger participants, use gentle words. Let them know that when we hurt inside, sometimes we act out or shut down. God wants them to know it's okay to talk about pain. They can go to safe people—and to Jesus—who will never turn them away.

Closing Prayer

Lord Jesus,
Thank You that You see our pain, even the pain we've carried in silence. Like the bleeding woman, we sometimes feel hopeless or ashamed, but You never turn us away. You call us Your sons and daughters, and You invite us to reach out to You in faith. Today we bring You the wounds, the addictions, and the struggles we cannot fix on our own. Break the cycle of pain in our lives and replace it with Your healing and peace. Restore our dignity, remind us of our worth, and help us to walk forward in freedom. We choose to trust You with our pain and believe that Your love is greater than anything that has tried to bind us. In Your precious name we pray, Amen.

Author's Note

Janet shares that her pain often led her into cycles of addiction. She explains that addiction is not only about substances—it can include sex, co-dependency, drugs, drinking, food, or even people-pleasing. These coping patterns promised relief but only brought shame and emptiness. After becoming a Christian, she learned that true healing comes when pain is brought to Jesus instead of hidden or numbed. She testifies that God broke the cycle of addiction in her life by meeting her pain with His love. Today, she encourages others to reach out in faith to Christ, who restores dignity, renews worth, and replaces the pain cycle with freedom.

Excerpt adapted with permission from Janet Marie Napper's personal story, ***Overcoming Abuse God's Way: Rags to Riches.***

Lesson 7: Fear

Introduction

Fear is one of the most powerful emotions survivors of abuse face. It creeps in when trust has been broken, when danger feels close, or when the future seems uncertain. Fear can paralyze us, keeping us from stepping into freedom. But God's Word reminds us that fear does not have the final say—His presence does. He promises to be our protector, our refuge, and our peace.

Biblical Foundation: Hagar in the Wilderness (Genesis 21)

Hagar, the servant of Sarah, experienced fear and despair when she and her son Ishmael were sent away into the desert. With no water left, Hagar placed Ishmael under a bush, unable to watch him die. In her greatest fear, God showed up. He called to her, reassured her, and provided what she needed. Hagar discovered that God saw her, heard her cries, and was present in her fear.

Scripture (NLT)

"When the water was gone, she put the boy in the shade of a bush. Then she went and sat down by herself about a hundred yards away. 'I don't want to watch the boy die,' she said, as she burst into tears. But God heard the boy crying, and the angel of God called to Hagar from heaven, 'Hagar, what's wrong? Do not be afraid! God has heard the boy crying as he lies there. Go to him and comfort him, for I will make a great nation from his descendants.' Then God opened Hagar's eyes, and she saw a well full of water."
– Genesis 21:15–19 (NLT)

"For God has not given us a spirit of fear and timidity, but of power, love, and self-discipline."
– 2 Timothy 1:7 (NLT)

Life Application

Fear is a natural human response, but when it controls us, it keeps us bound. Abuse often plants deep-rooted fears—fear of people, fear of failure, fear of abandonment, or fear that the pain will never end. Like Hagar, many survivors feel alone in the wilderness. But God reminds us: *Do not be afraid. I am with you.*

Healing from fear means:

- **Recognizing fear's lies** – Fear tells us we are helpless, but God says we are more than conquerors through Him.
- **Renewing our mind** – By replacing fearful thoughts with God's promises, we break fear's power.
- **Resting in God's presence** – Fear loses its grip when we remember we are not alone.

Psalm 56:3 (NLT) says, *"But when I am afraid, I will put my trust in you."* Fear may still knock at the door, but we can choose not to let it rule our lives.

Group Discussion Questions

1. What kinds of fear has abuse created in your life (fear of people, rejection, abandonment, etc.)?
2. How does Hagar's story show God's compassion in the middle of fear?
3. What Scriptures or promises of God encourage you most when you feel afraid?
4. What practical steps can you take to overcome fear with faith this week?

Child-Sensitive Note

Explain fear in simple words: *"Fear is when you feel scared, worried, or alone."* Tell children that even people in the Bible felt afraid, like Hagar. Remind them: *"God says, 'Do not be afraid. I am with you.' He always sees you and will never leave you."* Encourage them to talk to a safe adult when they feel fear.

Closing Prayer

Heavenly Father,
Thank You that You are greater than our fears. Just as You comforted Hagar in the wilderness, comfort us when we feel alone or afraid. Lord, we confess that fear has controlled parts of our lives, but today we surrender it to You. Fill us with Your power, Your love, and a sound mind. Replace fear with faith, and anxiety with peace. Remind us

that You are our refuge and strength, an ever-present help in trouble. In Jesus' name, Amen.

Author's Note

Fear was one of Janet's constant companions during her years of abuse. The fear of being hurt, the fear of abandonment, the fear of never being good enough—it all felt overwhelming. She writes that fear often dictated her choices and made her feel powerless. But in her journey of healing, God's Word became her weapon against fear. Scriptures like 2 Timothy 1:7 reminded her that fear was not from God, but that He had given her power, love, and a sound mind. Janet testifies that courage is not the absence of fear, but the decision to trust God in the middle of it. Her life is evidence that God's perfect love truly casts out fear and leads His children into freedom.

Excerpt adapted with permission from Janet Marie Napper's personal story, ***Overcoming Abuse God's Way: Rags to Riches.***

Lesson 8: Rejection

Introduction

Rejection is especially painful because it attacks the very core of who we are. God created us to be loved, accepted, and valued, yet rejection sends the opposite message—that we are unwanted, unworthy, or unloved. Abuse often magnifies this pain, leaving scars of abandonment and mistrust. But God's Word declares that we are chosen, deeply loved, and never rejected by Him.

Biblical Foundation: Leah and the Samaritan Woman

- **Leah's Story (Genesis 29)** – Leah was given to Jacob in marriage through deception. He loved her sister Rachel but not Leah. Scripture says Leah was "unloved," and though she bore Jacob children, she still longed for his affection. Her story shows the sting of rejection within family and relationships.

- **The Samaritan Woman (John 4)** – This woman carried the shame of rejection after five failed marriages. She came to the well at midday, likely to avoid others. Yet Jesus met her there, offering living water and acceptance she had never known.

Scripture (NLT)

"So Jacob slept with Rachel, too, and he loved her much more than Leah. He then stayed and worked for Laban the additional seven years."
— Genesis 29:30 (NLT)

"The woman was surprised, for Jews refuse to have anything to do with Samaritans. She said to Jesus, 'You are a Jew, and I am a Samaritan woman. Why are you asking me for a drink?' Jesus replied, 'If you only knew the gift God has for you and who you are speaking to, you would ask me, and I would give you living water.'"
— John 4:9–10 (NLT)

Life Application

Rejection can shape behavior in destructive ways. Some survivors respond by trying harder to please people, while others push people away to avoid being hurt again.

Rejection can also lead to emotional numbness, performance-based living, or difficulty trusting God.

But God reminds us of our identity in Him:

- We are **loved** (Jeremiah 31:3).
- We are **chosen** (Ephesians 1:4).
- We are **His masterpiece** (Ephesians 2:10).

Leah's story shows us that people may reject us, but God sees and values us. The Samaritan woman's story shows us that even when society rejects us, Jesus meets us personally with love and acceptance. Healing from rejection means replacing the lies with God's truth about our worth.

Group Discussion Questions

1. How has rejection in your life made it difficult to feel loved or accepted?
2. In what ways do you relate to Leah's or the Samaritan woman's story?
3. How has rejection affected the way you relate to other people?
4. What Scriptures remind you that God has accepted and chosen you?

Child-Sensitive Note

Explain rejection gently: *"Rejection is when someone makes you feel like you don't matter or don't belong."* Tell children: *"Even if people hurt you that way, God never rejects you. He always says, 'You are mine, and I love you.'"* Encourage them to talk to safe adults who will remind them of their value.

Closing Prayer

Heavenly Father,
Thank You that You never reject us. You see us, You love us, and You call us Your own. Lord, heal the wounds of rejection in our hearts. Where we have believed lies about

being unwanted or unloved, replace them with Your truth. Teach us to walk in the confidence that we are chosen and cherished by You. Help us to forgive those who rejected us and to trust that Your acceptance is enough. In Jesus' name, Amen.

Author's Note

Janet shares that rejection marked many seasons of her life—from being overlooked as a child to being discarded in relationships. She writes that rejection left her striving for approval, fearful of abandonment, and hesitant to trust—even with God. But as she walked through healing, God's Word reminded her that she was chosen, accepted, and dearly loved. Janet testifies that while human rejection wounds deeply, God's acceptance restores completely. Today, she stands in the freedom of knowing that her worth is not based on who rejected her, but on the One who calls her His beloved daughter.

Excerpt adapted with permission from Janet Marie Napper's personal story, ***Overcoming Abuse God's Way: Rags to Riches.***

Lesson 9: Judging

Introduction

When we've been deeply hurt, it becomes easy to judge others—especially when we feel vulnerable, afraid, or insecure. Judging is a way of protecting ourselves, of avoiding our own pain, or of trying to feel better by looking down on others. But Scripture calls us to humility, compassion, and truth. Judging forgets that we, too, are only standing by God's grace.

Biblical Foundation: The Woman Caught in Adultery (John 8:1–11)

The religious leaders brought a woman caught in adultery before Jesus. They judged her harshly and demanded punishment. But Jesus turned the judgment back on them. 'Let the one who has never sinned throw the first stone,' He said. One by one, they walked away. Jesus did not excuse the woman's sin—but He offered mercy. He reminded everyone that we need grace.

"They kept demanding an answer, so he stood up again and said, 'All right, but let the one who has never sinned throw the first stone!'"
"Then he stooped down again and wrote in the dust. When the accusers heard this, they slipped away one by one… until only Jesus was left."
"Then Jesus stood up again and said to the woman, 'Where are your accusers? Didn't even one of them condemn you?'"
"No, Lord," she said. And Jesus said, "Neither do I. Go and sin no more."

– John 8:7–11 (NLT)

Life Application

Judging others often comes from pain. When we've been rejected, we may build a false sense of identity—thinking we're better than others just to feel safe or worthy. But this traps us in comparison and keeps us from loving like Jesus. We forget who and whose we are. Whether we're fresh from abuse or far into our healing journey, we all stand only because of God's mercy.

Jesus said, 'He who humbles himself will be lifted up.' (Luke 18:14). True freedom comes not from pride, but from grace.

Warning Signs of Judgmentalism
- Constantly noticing others' faults
- Difficulty admitting when you're wrong
- Assuming others' motives without understanding their story
- Feeling superior or more spiritual than others
- Harsh opinions about people who sin differently from you
- Refusing to forgive or move on

Practical Steps to Overcome Judging
1. Acknowledge your pain – Judging often comes from unresolved wounds.
2. Remember God's grace – Reflect on where He brought you from.
3. Choose empathy – Try to understand others before labeling them.
4. Speak life – Replace criticism with encouragement.
5. Let go of needing to feel 'better than' – Let God define your worth.

Judging vs. Discernment
Jesus said, 'You will know them by their fruit.' (Matthew 7:16). It's not judgmental to evaluate someone's behavior for safety. But we must do it with love and wisdom, not pride or fear. The Fruit of the Spirit—love, joy, peace, patience, kindness, goodness, faithfulness, gentleness, and self-control—can guide us in relationships.

Helpful Scriptures (NLT)
"God opposes the proud but gives grace to the humble." – James 4:6

"Do not judge others, and you will not be judged." – Matthew 7:1

"You will know them by their fruits." – Matthew 7:16

"Let us not become conceited, or provoke one another, or be jealous of one another." – Galatians 5:26

Group Discussion Questions

1. Have you ever judged someone because it made you feel safer or better?

2. What does Jesus' response in this story teach you about mercy and grace?

3. What judgmental patterns do you recognize in yourself?

4. How can the Fruit of the Spirit guide you in choosing safe, loving relationships?

Child-Sensitive Note

Help children understand that judging others can hurt people and make us feel far from God. Instead, teach them to notice kind actions and good choices. Encourage them to ask God to help them be kind and understanding when others make mistakes.

Closing Prayer

Merciful Father,

Thank You for reminding us through Jesus' example that mercy triumphs over judgment. We confess that sometimes we judge others out of our own hurt, fear, or insecurity. Forgive us, Lord, for the times we have spoken harshly, assumed the worst, or looked down on others. Teach us to see people as You see them—broken, but deeply loved and worthy of grace. Fill our hearts with humility and compassion, so that instead of casting stones, we extend kindness, encouragement, and understanding. May Your Spirit guide us to walk in truth and love, remembering always that we, too, stand only by Your grace. In Jesus' name, Amen.

Author Notes

Janet experienced judging others out of her own fear of rejection. To protect herself from being hurt again, she built walls and withdrew, believing that judging others would keep her safe. But instead of protection, it brought isolation. The very connection her heart longed for was never established because fear had taken the place of love.

Through prayer and God's Word, Janet learned that judgment is not our place—there is only one righteous Judge. We are called to love and accept people as they are, just as

Christ loves and accepts us. Healing came as she surrendered her need to be right and allowed God's love to soften her heart.

Now, instead of judging to self-preserve, she chooses compassion, remembering that her worth and acceptance come from the One who matters most—Jesus Christ.

Excerpt adapted with permission from Janet Marie Napper's personal story, **Overcoming Abuse God's Way: Rags to Riches.**

Lesson 10: Anger

Introduction

Anger is a God-given emotion. It is not sin in itself but part of our natural response to life. Scripture even says, *"Be angry, and do not sin"* (Ephesians 4:26). However, abuse can distort how we express anger. Survivors may either suppress it out of fear or release it in unhealthy ways. Understanding anger helps us see that it can either be destructive or healing—depending on whether we surrender it to God.

Biblical Foundation: Moses and the Rock (Numbers 20)

Moses grew frustrated with the constant complaints of the Israelites. In his anger, instead of speaking to the rock as God commanded, Moses struck it twice. Water still flowed, but Moses lost the privilege of entering the Promised Land. His story shows that anger, when mishandled, can have lasting consequences.

Scripture (NLT)

"'You and Aaron must take the staff and assemble the entire community. As the people watch, speak to the rock over there, and it will pour out its water. You will provide enough water from the rock to satisfy the whole community and their livestock.' So Moses did as he was told. He took the staff from the place where it was kept before the Lord. Then he and Aaron summoned the people to come and gather at the rock. 'Listen, you rebels!' he shouted. 'Must we bring you water from this rock?' Then Moses raised his hand and struck the rock twice with the staff, and water gushed out. So the entire community and their livestock drank their fill. But the Lord said to Moses and Aaron, 'Because you did not trust me enough to demonstrate my holiness to the people of Israel, you will not lead them into the land I am giving them!'"
– Numbers 20:8–12 (NLT)

Life Application

- **Anger as an emotion** – Emotions are mood responses, often triggered by our thoughts. Abuse plants painful memories that can resurface as anger in the present.

- **Healing the root** – Renewing our minds with God's truth helps prevent past hurts from controlling present reactions.
- **Stages of Anger** –
    1. Irritation
    2. Frustration
    3. Hostility
    4. Rage
    Understanding where we are on this scale helps us stop anger before it controls us.
- **Forgiveness and anger** – Forgiveness is key to overcoming anger. Unforgiveness fuels resentment, but forgiveness releases us from the cycle of pain.

Anger is not only about others. Survivors often need to forgive themselves for words spoken in pain, or for times they withheld words of love and affirmation. Healing means allowing God to turn anger into a doorway for forgiveness, freedom, and peace.

Group Discussion Questions

1. How has anger shown up in your life as a result of abuse?
2. Which stage of anger (irritation, frustration, hostility, rage) do you most often experience?
3. How does Moses' story show the consequences of mismanaged anger?
4. What role does forgiveness play in releasing anger?

Child-Sensitive Note

Explain anger simply: *"Anger is when you feel upset inside and want to yell, cry, or hit. Everyone feels anger sometimes, even people in the Bible."* Teach children that anger itself isn't bad, but hurting others or themselves is wrong. Tell them: *"When you feel angry, talk to God and a safe adult. God can help you calm down and feel better."*

Closing Prayer

Lord God,

Thank You for giving us emotions, including anger. We confess that anger has often controlled us or hurt us because of our past pain. Heal the wounds that fuel our anger. Teach us to recognize when anger rises and to respond with wisdom instead of destruction. Help us forgive ourselves and others, releasing bitterness and choosing peace. Thank You for Your patience with us and for giving us the power of Your Spirit to walk in self-control. In Jesus' name, Amen.

Author's Note

As a child, Janet carried deep anger born from the pain of abuse. Afraid of rejection or punishment, she often bottled it up inside, only to have it erupt in ways that left her feeling ashamed and guilty. The unresolved hurt kept her trapped in a cycle of regret and self-blame.

Over time, God gently showed her that anger itself was not the enemy—unforgiveness was. As she learned to forgive both herself and those who had hurt her, the weight of anger began to lift.

Today, she testifies that anger no longer controls her; instead, God's peace rules her heart. Her journey shows that when anger is surrendered to God, it can become the doorway to forgiveness, freedom, and true healing.

Excerpt adapted with permission from Janet Marie Napper's personal story, **Overcoming Abuse God's Way: Rags to Riches.**

Lesson 11: Forgiveness

Introduction

Forgiveness is one of the hardest steps for survivors of abuse, yet it is also one of the most freeing. Many fear that forgiving means excusing the abuse or forgetting the pain. But forgiveness does not mean approving of what happened—it means releasing the burden of bitterness and entrusting justice to God. Forgiveness allows us to be free from the prison of anger, resentment, and shame.

Biblical Foundation: Joseph and His Brothers (Genesis 50)

Joseph was betrayed by his own brothers, sold into slavery, and falsely accused. Yet when he rose to power in Egypt, he forgave those who had harmed him. His words show the heart of true forgiveness: recognizing that while others intended harm, God can bring redemption.

Scripture (NLT)

"But Joseph replied, 'Don't be afraid of me. Am I God, that I can punish you? You intended to harm me, but God intended it all for good. He brought me to this position so I could save the lives of many people.'"
– Genesis 50:19–20 (NLT)

"Make allowance for each other's faults, and forgive anyone who offends you. Remember, the Lord forgave you, so you must forgive others."
– Colossians 3:13 (NLT)

Life Application

Forgiveness is not a one-time event but often a process. Survivors of abuse may need to forgive layer by layer, as new memories or emotions surface. Forgiveness does not excuse the abuser—it sets the survivor free.

Steps toward forgiveness:

1. **Acknowledge the hurt** – We cannot forgive what we deny.
2. **Release the offender to God** – Trust Him as the righteous Judge.
3. **Choose freedom over bitterness** – Bitterness chains us to the past; forgiveness opens the door to healing.
4. **Forgive yourself** – Many survivors carry misplaced guilt or regret. God offers complete forgiveness through Christ.

Joseph's story shows us that forgiveness transforms suffering into testimony. What was meant for destruction can become a story of God's redemption.

Group Discussion Questions

1. What fears or misconceptions have made forgiveness difficult for you?
2. How does Joseph's story encourage you about the power of forgiveness?
3. How do you think forgiving others affects your ability to heal?
4. Is there an area where you need to forgive yourself?

Child-Sensitive Note

Explain forgiveness simply: *"Forgiveness means letting go of the hurt someone caused you. It doesn't mean what they did was okay, but it means you don't let the hurt stay in your heart."* Tell children: *"God always forgives us, and He helps us forgive others so our hearts can be light and free."*

Closing Prayer

Merciful Father,
Thank You for forgiving us completely through Jesus Christ. Lord, we admit that

forgiveness is hard, especially when the wounds are deep. Give us the strength to release those who hurt us and to trust You with justice. Heal our hearts where bitterness has taken root. Teach us also to forgive ourselves, knowing that Your grace is enough. May we walk in the freedom that comes from forgiving, just as we have been forgiven. In Jesus' name, Amen.

Author's Note

Janet shares that for years, she believed forgiving meant pretending the abuse never happened. As a teenager, she carried the heavy weight of anger, not understanding why she couldn't break free. It wasn't until God revealed that forgiveness wasn't about excusing the abuser—it was about setting herself free—that her healing began.

Through prayer and God's Word, she learned to release those who had hurt her and to forgive herself for carrying shame that was never hers to bear. She also had to forgive her family for misunderstanding her, for the gossip about her, and for the birthday cards and phone calls that never came. She realized that holding on to unforgiveness only kept her trapped in the pain, but choosing forgiveness unlocked true freedom.

Today, she testifies that forgiveness was the key that opened the door to her healing. Her story is a powerful reminder that God's grace can heal even the deepest wounds.

Excerpt adapted with permission from Janet Marie Napper's personal story, ***Overcoming Abuse God's Way: Rags to Riches.***

Lesson 12: Loving Others & Blended Families

Introduction

To love others well, we must first know we are loved by God. Abuse often distorts our understanding of love, leaving us insecure, fearful, or dependent on others for worth. In blended families, the challenges can be even greater children did not invite a new parent into their lives, and adults may carry wounds from past relationships. Without the foundation of God's love, our attempts to love can fall short. With His love, we can extend patience, grace, and healing to those around us.

Biblical Foundation: Mary, Martha, and Lazarus (John 11)

When Lazarus died, Mary and Martha questioned Jesus' love: *"Lord, if you had been here, my brother would not have died."* Their grief revealed how pain can cloud our understanding of God's love. Yet Jesus wept with them and then raised Lazarus from the dead—proving His love is constant, even when circumstances are painful.

Scripture (NLT)

"When Jesus saw her weeping and saw the other people wailing with her, a deep anger welled up within him, and he was deeply troubled. 'Where have you put him?' he asked them. They told him, 'Lord, come and see.' Then Jesus wept."
– John 11:33–35 (NLT)

"Dear friends, let us continue to love one another, for love comes from God. Anyone who loves is a child of God and knows God. But anyone who does not love does not know God, for God is love."
– 1 John 4:7–8 (NLT)

Life Application

- **Knowing we are loved** – Without experiencing God's love, we may try to get it from others in unhealthy ways. Abuse can make us doubt love altogether. God's love is the only perfect love, one that never fails.

- **Blended families** – Children in blended families may feel insecure, rejected, or overlooked. They need consistent love and reassurance. Adults, too, must learn to show love selflessly, even when faced with challenges.
- **Redefining love** – True love is not about expecting others to meet our needs in the way we want. It is about showing patience, kindness, and sacrifice, as Christ has shown us.

Mary and Martha questioned Jesus' love, yet He proved it through His actions. In the same way, love in families—especially blended families—must be more than words; it must be demonstrated through grace, forgiveness, and care.

Group Discussion Questions

1. How has abuse affected your ability to understand or accept love?
2. Why is it hard for children in blended families to feel secure in love?
3. How does Jesus' love for Mary, Martha, and Lazarus encourage you in your relationships?
4. What practical ways can you show God's love in your family today?

Child-Sensitive Note

Explain love simply: *"Love means caring for someone in a safe way that helps them feel special and important."* Remind children that God's love is perfect and never changes, even if people sometimes fail to love well. For blended families, explain gently: *"It's okay to have different feelings when new people join the family, but God wants everyone to feel safe and loved."*

Closing Prayer

Heavenly Father,
Thank You for loving us with a perfect love that never fails. Heal the places where abuse

or rejection has damaged our understanding of love. Teach us to receive Your love fully, so that we can love others from a place of security. Bless blended families with patience, kindness, and grace. Help parents and children to understand one another and to reflect Your love in their homes. Thank You that Your love covers every wound and restores every heart. In Jesus' name, Amen.

Author's Note

Janet shares that for years, she struggled to grasp the meaning of real love. Abuse had taught her that love was conditional, inconsistent, or unsafe. When she entered the challenges of blended family life, those wounds often resurfaced.

She came to realize that blended families can be a blessing when you choose to see them as an opportunity to love your spouse and their children unconditionally with the love of God—even if that love is not immediately received. Over time, and through prayer, Janet became free from the pain she once carried in her blended family.

Through God's healing, she learned that His love is the foundation for all relationships. She discovered that when children are shown security, patience, and unconditional care, they begin to understand God's love. Janet testifies that her journey of learning to love others began with learning how deeply she was loved by her heavenly Father.

Excerpt adapted with permission from Janet Marie Napper's personal story, **Overcoming Abuse God's Way: Rags to Riches.**

Lesson 13: Co-dependency

Introduction

Co-dependency is when a person becomes overly reliant on others for their identity, worth, or happiness. Survivors of abuse often fall into co-dependency, believing they must please others to be accepted or loved. While helping others is good, co-dependency crosses a line—it keeps us bound by people's approval instead of living in God's freedom. True healing comes when we depend on God first, rather than on people for our value.

Biblical Foundation: Martha and Mary (Luke 10)

Martha was distracted by serving and worried about pleasing others, while Mary sat at Jesus' feet, receiving His love and truth. Martha's frustration reveals how co-dependency can leave us stressed and unfulfilled, while Mary's example reminds us that intimacy with Christ comes first.

Scripture (NLT)

"But Martha was distracted by the big dinner she was preparing. She came to Jesus and said, 'Lord, doesn't it seem unfair to you that my sister just sits here while I do all the work? Tell her to come and help me.' But the Lord said to her, 'My dear Martha, you are worried and upset over all these details! There is only one thing worth being concerned about. Mary has discovered it, and it will not be taken away from her.'"
– Luke 10:40–42 (NLT)

"It is better to take refuge in the Lord than to trust in people."
– Psalm 118:8 (NLT)

Life Application

Co-dependency can look like:

- Always saying "yes" to avoid disappointing others.
- Feeling responsible for other people's happiness.
- Believing your worth comes from what you do, not who you are.

- Fearing rejection so much that you lose yourself in relationships.

Abuse often trains survivors to be "people-pleasers" to avoid conflict or gain acceptance. But God never intended for us to live this way. He calls us to put Him first and find our security in His love.

Steps to Overcome Co-dependency God's Way:

1. **Identify unhealthy patterns** – Recognize where people's approval has more power than God's truth.
2. **Renew your mind** – Replace the lie, *"I must keep everyone happy to be loved,"* with God's promise: *"I am already loved and chosen."*
3. **Set healthy boundaries** – Love others without losing yourself.
4. **Depend on God first** – Seek His approval above anyone else's.

When we let go of co-dependency, we gain true freedom: the ability to love people without being controlled by them.

Group Discussion Questions

1. How has co-dependency (people-pleasing, fear of rejection, etc.) shown up in your life?
2. Why do you think survivors of abuse are especially vulnerable to co-dependency?
3. How does Mary's example of sitting at Jesus' feet show a better way to live?
4. What step can you take this week to depend more on God than on people?

Child-Sensitive Note

Explain simply: *"Co-dependency is when we try too hard to make people happy because we are afraid they won't love us if we don't."* Tell children: *"God wants you to know you are loved just as you are. You don't have to earn His love or anyone else's. Being kind is good, but you don't have to lose yourself to please others."*

Closing Prayer

Gracious Father,

Thank You that our value does not come from what others think, but from who You say we are. Lord, we confess that at times we have lived to please people instead of You. Break the chains of co-dependency in our lives. Teach us to set healthy boundaries, to find our worth in Your love, and to walk in the freedom Christ purchased for us. Help us love others from a place of strength, not fear. In Jesus' name, Amen.

Author's Note

Those who have been rejected as children often grow up depending on others to love them. When they do not experience that unconditional love, they try to make a way to get loved. Most of the time, that love is not authentic and only keeps the person dependent on more and more people, increasingly doing so to have that need for love met. Even though they may sense it is false, they cling to it, which leaves them feeling lonely and empty inside.

Janet shares that this cycle of co-dependency ruled much of her life after abuse. She felt she had to keep everyone happy or risk being rejected again. This left her exhausted, fearful, and uncertain of her own worth.

Over time, God gently showed her that her value was not in what she did for others, but in who she was as His beloved child. Learning to depend on God first became one of the most freeing parts of her healing journey. Today, she testifies that she no longer lives for the approval of others—she lives for the smile of her Heavenly Father, and in that freedom, she can love others without losing herself.

Excerpt adapted with permission from Janet Marie Napper's personal story, ***Overcoming Abuse God's Way: Rags to Riches.***

Lesson 14: Romance & Sexual Addiction

Introduction

Romance and sexual addictions are powerful traps for many survivors of abuse. These addictions often grow from a false belief that *sex equals love* or that relationships will heal our emptiness. Abuse distorts intimacy, leaving wounds that seek comfort in familiar but destructive patterns. Instead of feeling loved, these addictions leave survivors feeling used, ashamed, and broken. But God's Word offers freedom, dignity, and protection through His standards of purity and true love.

Biblical Foundation: The Woman at the Well (John 4)

The Samaritan woman had been married five times and was living with a man who was not her husband. She likely sought love and security but found herself caught in a cycle of rejection and shame. Jesus met her with compassion, not condemnation, offering her living water that would satisfy the deepest thirst of her soul.

Scripture (NLT)

"The woman was surprised, for Jews refuse to have anything to do with Samaritans. She said to Jesus, 'You are a Jew, and I am a Samaritan woman. Why are you asking me for a drink?' Jesus replied, 'If you only knew the gift God has for you and who you are speaking to, you would ask me, and I would give you living water.'"
– John 4:9–10 (NLT)

"'Anyone who drinks this water will soon become thirsty again. But those who drink the water I give will never be thirsty again. It becomes a fresh, bubbling spring within them, giving them eternal life.'"
– John 4:13–14 (NLT)

Life Application

Abuse often leaves survivors with broken confidence and unmet needs. Romance or sexual addiction may feel like an escape but only deepens emptiness. Triggers like movies, songs, voices, or even loneliness can feed the cycle, keeping survivors trapped.

The Cycle of Romance Addiction:

1. **Trigger** – A memory, loneliness, song, movie, or voice stirs desire.
2. **Plot or Plan** – Instead of taking the trigger to God in prayer, the mind begins planning how to feed the addiction.
3. **Preparation** – Dressing for attention or going to places where the addiction can be fulfilled.
4. **Temporary Relief** – Acting on the addiction creates a false sense of comfort.
5. **Reality** – Afterward, shame and regret set in.
6. **Self-Abuse** – Speaking harsh or condemning words about yourself.
7. **Depression** – Falling into sadness and hopelessness.
8. **Empty Promises** – Saying, *"I'll never do this again,"* but repeating the cycle because there is no support and no surrender to God's way of healing.

This cycle can feel impossible to break, but God offers freedom through His Spirit, His Word, and healthy support from others.

Key truths for healing:

- **Love ≠ Sex** – Love is patient, kind, and unselfish (1 Corinthians 13). Abuse teaches the opposite.
- **Addiction leaves us empty** – After the thrill fades, shame grows. Only God's love satisfies.
- **Healing requires separation** – Breaking free often means creating distance from unhealthy relationships, media, or environments that fuel the addiction.
- **God's standards protect** – Purity is not punishment but protection, guarding our hearts and restoring our dignity.

The Samaritan woman's encounter with Jesus shows that no cycle of addiction is too strong for His love to break. He offers living water—true intimacy with God—that fills the emptiness no relationship or addiction can satisfy.

Group Discussion Questions

1. Why do you think survivors of abuse are especially vulnerable to romance or sexual addictions?
2. What lies have you believed about love and sex, and how does God's Word correct them?
3. What can we learn from the Samaritan woman's story about God's compassion for those trapped in cycles of shame?
4. What practical steps (boundaries, accountability, prayer) can help break free from these addictions?

Child-Sensitive Note

When teaching younger teens, explain simply: *"Sometimes people who have been hurt look for love in the wrong places. They might confuse love with things that don't really mean love at all. But God's love is safe, pure, and lasting."* Emphasize that God values their body and their heart, and that His love never uses or hurts.

Closing Prayer

Heavenly Father,
Thank You for seeing us even in our struggles with romance or sexual addiction. Lord, we confess that sometimes we look for love in the wrong places. Heal the wounds that drive us toward false intimacy. Break the chains of addiction and set us free in Your truth. Help us to separate from anything that triggers shame or emptiness, and instead draw us to the living water of Your love. Restore our confidence, dignity, and purity as Your beloved children. In Jesus' name, Amen.

Author's Note

Janet shares that because of early abuse, she struggled with the lie that love and sex were the same. This lie made her vulnerable to romance addiction, drawing her into relationships that felt familiar but left her emptier than before. She describes how the cycle repeated itself—triggers, planning, false comfort, regret, self-condemnation, depression, and empty promises to "never do it again." What finally broke the cycle was learning to surrender her triggers to God, surround herself with Christ-centered support, and let His truth define her worth. Today, she testifies that God's standards are not restrictive—they are protective, restoring dignity and leading His children into freedom.

Excerpt adapted with permission from Janet Marie Napper's personal story, ***Overcoming Abuse God's Way: Rags to Riches.***

Lesson 15: Generational Patterns & Ancestral Sin

Introduction

Generational patterns are behaviors, sins, and wounds passed down through families. Abuse, addiction, anger, rejection, and fear often run in cycles—shaping children the same way parents or caregivers were shaped. Until someone breaks the cycle through God's truth, these patterns continue. The Bible also warns about ancestral sins, where past generations open doors to demonic influence. But the good news is this: through Jesus Christ, we can be set free. God's Word renews our minds, His Spirit gives us strength, and His armor protects us from spiritual attacks.

Biblical Foundation: Israel's Struggle and Jesus' Healing Power

Throughout Israel's history, people often repeated the sins of their fathers. Yet God continually called them back. Jesus came to demonstrate that God is *for us, not against us.* He healed the sick, fed the hungry, cast out demons, and loved the outcasts—showing that God's power is stronger than every generational curse.

Scripture (NLT)

On Demonic Influence and Ancestral Sin:

- "I will also turn against those who commit spiritual prostitution by putting their trust in mediums or in those who consult the spirits of the dead. I will cut them off from the community." – Leviticus 20:6 (NLT)

- "Do not defile yourselves by turning to mediums or to those who consult the spirits of the dead. I am the Lord your God." – Leviticus 19:31 (NLT)

- "Do not let your people practice fortune-telling, or use sorcery, or interpret omens, or engage in witchcraft, or cast spells, or function as mediums or psychics, or call forth the spirits of the dead." – Deuteronomy 18:10–11 (NLT)

- "They worshiped their idols, which led to their downfall. They even sacrificed their sons and their daughters to the demons." – Psalm 106:36–37 (NLT)

On Spiritual Warfare:

"For we are not fighting against flesh-and-blood enemies, but against evil rulers and authorities of the unseen world, against mighty powers in this dark world, and against evil spirits in the heavenly places."
– Ephesians 6:12 (NLT)

"Put on all of God's armor so that you will be able to stand firm against all strategies of the devil."
– Ephesians 6:11 (NLT)

Life Application

Generational patterns teach us to live out what we've seen modeled. A child who grows up in anger often struggles with anger. A child who grows up in addiction often battles addiction themselves. Demonic influence exploits these patterns, keeping families in bondage.

But God's Word and His Spirit give us the power to break these cycles. We are not bound by our past—we are made new in Christ.

The Armor of God (Ephesians 6:13–18):

1. **Belt of Truth** – God's truth breaks generational lies.
2. **Breastplate of Righteousness** – Protects our hearts from shame and guilt.
3. **Shoes of Peace** – Gives us stability in a world of family conflict.
4. **Shield of Faith** – Deflects the fiery arrows of generational doubt, fear, and attack.
5. **Helmet of Salvation** – Guards our minds against lies of the enemy.
6. **Sword of the Spirit** – God's Word defeats demonic deception.
7. **Prayer** – Our lifeline of strength, authority, and power.

Breaking generational sin requires courage, prayer, and trust in God's promises. Through Christ, we can stop cycles of abuse and start a new legacy of healing and hope.

Group Discussion Questions

1. What generational patterns have you noticed in your family line (abuse, addiction, fear, etc.)?
2. How does knowing Jesus is *for you* encourage you to break these cycles?
3. Which piece of the armor of God do you most need to put on today?
4. How can you begin creating a new spiritual legacy for your family?

Child-Sensitive Note

Explain simply: *"Sometimes families pass down habits or hurts, like anger, fear, or not knowing how to love well. But God can help us stop those patterns."* Encourage children: *"You don't have to be like your parents or grandparents if they made wrong choices. God can help you make new, healthy choices."*

Closing Prayer

Heavenly Father,
Thank You that in Christ, we are no longer bound by generational sin or family patterns of pain. Lord, reveal to us the cycles that need to be broken. Protect us from demonic influence and renew our minds with Your truth. Help us put on the full armor of God every day and stand firm in Your strength. Thank You for giving us a new identity and a new legacy in Christ. In Jesus' mighty name, Amen.

Author's Note

Janet shares that one of the generational patterns she observed came from her foster parents. She observed how manipulation was used to achieve desired outcomes or necessities, and how insensitivity toward others became a way of life. Without realizing it, she carried some of these patterns into adulthood. After becoming a Christian, God began to show her these unhealthy behaviors and taught her to live differently, choosing truth over manipulation, and compassion over insensitivity. She testifies that while generational patterns can shape us, God's Spirit can retrain us. Through His power, cycles can be broken and replaced with love, honesty, and grace.

Excerpt adapted with permission from Janet Marie Napper's personal story, ***Overcoming Abuse God's Way: Rags to Riches.***

Lesson 16: Root Strongholds and Soul Ties

What Are Root Strongholds?

Root strongholds are deeply rooted mindsets, behaviors, and spiritual influences that resist God's truth. These strongholds often develop through trauma, family patterns, sinful habits, or emotional wounds. They are fortified by lies and demonic influences meant to keep us bound and disconnected from God's purpose and love.

Spiritual Discernment Exercise: Breaking Familiar Strongholds

Note: We all struggle a little here and there—that's part of being human. But root strongholds are the deeper, repeated struggles that keep us bound to a thing (a thought, habit, fear, or relationship pattern), even when we want to change. They're often fueled by old wounds, lies we've believed, or repeated sin.

As we grow in Christ, we are being transformed by the Holy Spirit from glory to glory (2 Corinthians 3:18). This means the Lord doesn't just expose our strongholds—He helps us overcome them step by step, making us more like Jesus each day.

Life Application: Breaking Root Strongholds

Strongholds are like weeds—if you only cut them at the surface, they will grow back. To truly overcome them, you must allow God to go to the root and replace the lies with His truth. This process isn't about trying harder; it's about surrendering deeper.

1. **Identify the Root**
   Ask the Holy Spirit to reveal the root of the stronghold in your life. Is it fear, rejection, unforgiveness, anger, or a destructive relationship? Write it down in your journal.
2. **Replace the Lie with Truth**
   Every stronghold is fortified by a lie. Once you recognize the lie (for example, *"I'm worthless,"* or *"I'll always be this way"*), replace it with God's truth from Scripture (for example, *"I am God's masterpiece"* – Ephesians 2:10).
3. **Renounce and Break Agreement**
   Out loud, renounce the lie and any agreement you've made with it. Example: *"In Jesus' name, I renounce the lie that I am worthless. I agree with God's Word that I am loved, chosen, and valuable."*
4. **Establish New Patterns**
   Begin to walk in the opposite spirit. If your stronghold was fear, practice stepping

out in faith. If it was rejection, start reaching out to others in love. Transformation happens as you choose God's way in daily life.
5. **Stay Accountable**
Share your journey with a trusted believer, mentor, or support group. Strongholds lose their power when brought into the light.

Key Scripture (NLT):
"We use God's mighty weapons, not worldly weapons, to knock down the strongholds of human reasoning and to destroy false arguments. We destroy every proud obstacle that keeps people from knowing God. We capture their rebellious thoughts and teach them to obey Christ." — 2 Corinthians 10:4–5

From Bondage to Freedom: Steps for Healing

Take time to pray and ask the Holy Spirit to reveal strongholds that have passed through your family or entered through trauma or sin. **Circle** anything in the lists below that you've personally struggled with or seen in your parents, siblings, or people you've been sexually involved with.

(This exercise is for freedom, not shame. As the Lord reveals a root, invite His truth to replace the lie, and ask for next steps—repentance, boundaries, accountability, or healing prayer.)

Key Scriptures for Renouncing Strongholds

2 Corinthians 10:4-5 – "We use God's mighty weapons... to knock down the strongholds of human reasoning..." (NLT)

Luke 10:19 – "Look, I have given you authority over all the power of the enemy..." (NLT)

Revelation 12:11 – "And they have defeated him by the blood of the Lamb and by their testimony..." (NLT)

Romans 8:17 – "And since we are his children, we are his heirs..." (NLT)

Root Strongholds and Related Spirits

1. Stronghold of Fear (2 Tim 1:7)

    - Nightmares
    - Timidity/Shyness
    - Any kind of Fear
    - Phobias
    - Worry/Anxiety
    - Inferiority
    - Performance
    - Overly Critical
    - Mental Illness

2. Stronghold of Divination (Acts 16:16-18)

    - Witchcraft
    - Astrology/Horoscopes
    - Satanism
    - Rebellion/Stubbornness
    - Secret Organizations
    - False Gods

3. Stronghold of Harlotry (Lev 19:29)

    - Adultery
    - Incest
    - Molestation/Rape
    - Lust
    - Idolatry
    - Pornography
    - Masturbation
    - Prostitution

4. **Stronghold of Bondage (Rom 8:15)**

    - Cigarettes
    - Alcohol
    - Drugs
    - Workaholic
    - Superiority
    - Addicted to Another Person
    - Computer/Internet
    - Food
    - Soul Ties

5. **Stronghold of Haughtiness (Prov 16:18-19)**

    - Pride
    - Mockery
    - Scorn
    - Judgment
    - Rudeness
    - Bragging
    - Superiority
    - Egotism
    - Arrogance
    - Stubbornness
    - Contention
    - Gossip
    - Prejudice
    - Overbearing
    - Domineering
    - Self-Righteousness
    - Controlling
    - Criticism
    - Independence

6. Stronghold of Perverseness (Isaiah 19:14)

- Any Sexual Deviation
- Unreasonableness
- Abnormal Crankiness
- False Teachers
- Witchcraft
- Self-Lovers

7. Stronghold of Antichrist (1 John 4:3)

- Attempts to take place of Christ
- Opposes the Bible
- Opposes Christ's Deity
- Persecutes Believers
- Atheism

8. Stronghold of Heaviness (Isaiah 61:3)

- Depression
- Discouragement
- Self-Pity
- Gloominess
- Defilement
- Loneliness
- Unjustified Guilt
- Victim Mentality
- Rejection
- Abnormal Grief
- Broken Heart
- Whining
- Despair
- Hopelessness
- Shame
- Humiliation

9. Stronghold of Lying (2 Chron 18:22)

- Lies
- Deception
- Flattery
- Strong Delusions
- Excessive Talking
- Profanity
- Religious Stronghold
- Condemnation
- Vain Imaginations
- Daydreaming
- Performance
- Financial Problems
- Exaggeration
- Hypocrisy
- Emotionalism

10. Stronghold of Jealousy (Numbers 5:14)

- Jealousy
- Cruelty
- Revenge
- Suspicion
- Distrustfulness
- Insecurity
- Competition
- Self-Centeredness
- Hard Heartedness
- Divorce
- Division
- Anger
- Murder
- Rage
- Hatred

11. Stronghold of Stupor (Romans 11:8)

- Constant Fatigue
- Passivity
- Procrastination
- Self-Pity
- Blocks Success
- Withdraws from Life
- Spiritual Slumber

12. Stronghold of Error (1 John 4:6)

- Irresponsibility
- Immaturity
- Inappropriate Thinking
- Confusion
- Eating Disorders
- Wrong Decisions
- Doubt
- Deception
- Cults
- False Preachers/Prophets
- Racism
- Intellectualism
- Compromise

13. Stronghold of Death (Hebrews 2:14-15)

- Patterns of Death

14. Stronghold of Jezebel (Revelation 2:20)

- Manipulation
- Unreasonable
- Unyielding
- Unteachable
- Infallible
- Twisting Scripture

- Hyper-Spiritual
- No Accountability
- Religious Spirit
- Family Disorder
- Looks to Others, not Husband

Soul Ties and Biblical Warnings

Even though the Bible does not directly use the phrase "soul ties" and there is no scientific proof of them, the concept is often used to describe the deep emotional and spiritual bonds formed through close relationships—especially sexual, abusive, or manipulative ones. These bonds can have a lasting influence unless broken through repentance, healing, and prayer.

Scriptural Warnings About Unhealthy Attachments

2 Corinthians 11:20 (NLT): "You put up with it when someone enslaves you, takes everything you have, takes advantage of you, takes control of everything, and slaps you in the face."
Reflects the control and unhealthy dominance that can accompany ungodly relational bonds.

Proverbs 6:32 (NLT): "But the man who commits adultery is an utter fool, for he destroys himself."
Shows how sexual sin creates destructive consequences, including harmful relational entanglements.

1 Corinthians 6:16 (NLT): "And don't you realize that if a man joins himself to a prostitute, he becomes one body with her? For the Scriptures say, 'The two are united into one.'"
Reveals the spiritual binding that occurs through sexual union, pointing to the seriousness of intimacy outside God's design.

Steps to Break Free from a Soul Tie

1. Acknowledge the Tie

Ask the Holy Spirit to reveal any unhealthy bond that keeps you tied to a person in ways that bring shame, pain, or control.

Be honest about the relationship and its impact on you. Naming it is the first step to breaking its power.

2. **Repent and Renounce**

Repent for any sin connected to the relationship (sexual sin, idolatry, control, etc.).

Renounce the soul tie out loud in prayer, breaking agreement with it:
"In the name of Jesus, I renounce every unhealthy tie to [person's name]. I break every chain of shame, fear, control, or desire that does not come from God. My soul belongs to Jesus Christ alone."

3. **Forgive and Release**

Forgive the person for the harm they caused (whether abuse, betrayal, or abandonment).

Forgiveness doesn't excuse their behavior—it frees you from being bound to it.

Release them into God's hands. You are not their savior—Jesus is.

4. **Cut Off Access**

If possible, set healthy boundaries or go "no contact" with the person.

Remove physical reminders (gifts, photos, messages, mementos) that keep the bond alive.
Stop revisiting them emotionally through fantasy, memories, or social media.

5. **Replace the Lie with Truth**

Soul ties often convince us, "I can't live without them" or "They complete me."

Replace those lies with God's Word:

"I am complete in Christ" (Colossians 2:10).

"Whom the Son sets free is free indeed" (John 8:36).

"I belong to God" (1 Corinthians 6:19–20).

6. Seek Healing Prayer & Accountability

Ask trusted believers, pastors, or prayer partners to stand with you in prayer.

Breakthrough is often strengthened in community.

If abuse or trauma is involved, consider Christ-centered counseling.

7. Invite the Holy Spirit to Fill the Empty Space

Breaking a soul tie leaves a void—ask the Holy Spirit to fill it with His love, peace, and truth.

Pray daily for renewed thoughts, healed emotions, and strength to walk in freedom.

Prayer to Break a Soul Tie

Father God,
I come to You in the name of Jesus. I confess and repent of the relationship that created this soul tie. I renounce every unhealthy bond with [name] and break agreement with the lies, control, and addiction tied to it. By the authority of Jesus Christ, I break every chain, every spiritual influence, and every hold this tie has had on my life. I forgive [name] for the hurt they caused, and I release them into Your hands. Holy Spirit, heal my heart, renew my mind, and fill every empty place with Your love. My body, soul, and spirit belong to Jesus alone. Thank You for setting me free. In Jesus' name, Amen.

Author's Note

Janet experienced many layers of abuse, each one leaving behind emotional scars and unhealthy spiritual ties. To finalize her freedom, she had to acknowledge the truth about ungodly soul ties and renounce them in the name of Jesus with sincerity in her heart. Some of these ties were difficult to break because the relationships, though abusive, were also close and meaningful at times. This made the process painful and confusing.

Yet through prayer, God's Word, and the support of others, Janet learned to release those ties and entrust her heart fully to the Lord. As she surrendered, God faithfully cut away every unhealthy attachment, replacing bondage with freedom. This healing allowed her to discern unsafe people more clearly and to walk in God's protection and peace.

Excerpt adapted with permission from Janet Marie Napper's personal story, **Overcoming Abuse God's Way: Rags to Riches**

Congratulations on completing this journey through *Overcoming Abuse God's Way*. Finishing this study is more than just completing lessons—it is a courageous step toward healing, freedom, and restoration. You have faced painful truths, welcomed God's Word into wounded places, and chosen to walk in His light instead of shame.

This is not the end of your story—it's the beginning of a new chapter. You are no longer defined by abuse, rejection, or fear. You are defined by God's love, which calls you chosen, beloved, and free. As you continue to grow, remember that healing is a lifelong process, but with Christ, you are being renewed day by day.

It is also important to surround yourself with **like-minded, Christ-centered friends and community**. Seek out weekly support, accountability, and encouragement as you walk in God's love and healing. Ask the Lord to show you who around you can be a true source of strength, prayer, and support. Healing is not meant to be walked alone—God often sends others to walk beside us on the journey.

Your courage to complete this study is a testimony that hope is real, change is possible, and God's power to restore is greater than any wound of the past. May you walk forward with confidence, knowing that your story now carries hope for others who are still waiting for healing.

You are an overcomer. You are deeply loved. And your story is not over—it's just beginning.

Connect with OAGW

Web: www.oagw.world

Facebook page: Overcoming Abuse God's Way

Email: contact@oagw.world

WhatsApp: 00-1-901-605-8087

Resources

1. Christian Counseling and Trauma Recovery References

- Allender, Dan B. The Wounded Heart: Hope for Adult Victims of Childhood Sexual Abuse. NavPress, 2018.
- Cloud, Henry, and Townsend, John. Boundaries: When to Say Yes, How to Say No to Take Control of Your Life. Zondervan, 1992.
- Van der Kolk, Bessel A. The Body Keeps the Score: Brain, Mind, and Body in the Healing of Trauma. Penguin Books, 2015.
- Anderson, Neil T. The Bondage Breaker: Overcoming Negative Thoughts, Irrational Feelings, and Habitual Sins. Harvest House Publishers, 2019.
- Meyer, Joyce. Battlefield of the Mind: Winning the Battle in Your Mind. FaithWords, 2008.
- Stanley, Charles F. Emotions: Confront the Lies. Conquer with Truth. Thomas Nelson, 2012.
- Blackaby, Henry & Richard. Experiencing God: Knowing and Doing the Will of God. B&H Publishing, 2008.
- Crabb, Larry. Inside Out. NavPress, 1988.
- Seamands, David A. Healing for Damaged Emotions. David C. Cook, 1991.
- Celebrate Recovery Ministry Resources. Saddleback Church, Lake Forest, CA.

2. Faith-Based and Ministry Resources Consulted

- Celebrate Recovery Leader's Guide, Saddleback Church
- Healing the Wounds of Trauma: How the Church Can Help, American Bible Society, 2016
- Restoring the Foundations International, Healing and Deliverance Ministry
- Freedom in Christ Ministries, Neil T. Anderson
- American Association of Christian Counselors (AACC)
- First Nations Version: An Indigenous Translation of the New Testament, InterVarsity Press, 2021 (for contextual understanding in Lakota ministry work)

3. Author's Story & Testimony

Excerpts from Overcoming Abuse God's Way: Rags to Riches © Janet Marie Napper, used with permission of the author.

Personal Note from the Author

To all the Christian authors, teachers, and trainers who have gone before me—thank you. Your obedience to write, teach, and share your own stories of pain, redemption, and victory has shaped my journey and strengthened my calling.

Through your books, university lectures, online courses, webinars, and in-person training, I found guidance, knowledge, and the courage to grow.

Free and Fearless is not written from theory alone, but from transformation—mine, touched by your work. Each page carries traces of your faithfulness, your insight, and your example of living in victory through Christ.

Thank you for being vessels of truth and grace. Because of you, I was educated not just in the mind, but in the heart, learning that healing is possible, freedom is real, and God's love never fails.

With deepest gratitude and love,

— Janet Marie Napper

Made in the USA
Coppell, TX
18 February 2026